THE CHURCH IN
WINSCOMBE

Winscombe and Sandford
Millennium Series

1

CONTENTS

ACKNOWLEDGEMENTS

Many people have contributed to this publication: Frances Neale, Archivist to the Dean and Chapter of Wells Cathedral; Mick Aston, Professor of Landscape Archaeology at Bristol University; Dr Joe Bettey, Reader of Local History in Bristol University; and Reverend Bernard Salmon, Vicar of Winscombe 1971-1992. The illustrations are by Archie Forbes.

Thanks also to Susan Shaw, Sue Gunn, Roy Rice, David Bromwich, Gerald Lloyd, John Matthews, Geoff Luckett and Richard Neale.

Maria Forbes

Copyright © The Authors 2000

ISBN: 1 901 084 22 1

Printed by Woodspring Education Resource Centre, Lime Close, Locking BS24 8BB.

ILLUSTRATIONS AND PHOTOGRAPHS

INTRODUCTION

THE MANOR OF WINSCOMBE

In the Domesday Survey of 1086 "The Manor of Winescome" is included among the possessions of Glastonbury Abbey. Winscombe remained a possession of Glastonbury until the 13th century when it was handed over to Savaric, Bishop of Bath of Wells, even though the monks of the Abbey refused to recognise him as their head. When Savaric died in 1205 Glastonbury Abbey regained its independence but in return had to surrender various lands to Bishop Jocelyn, who was Savaric's successor. Subsequently, in 1239, Bishop Jocelyn gave the Manor of Winscombe to the Dean and Chapter of Wells Cathedral.

The Parish of Winscombe was made up of many separate settlements including: Nye, Sandford, Dinghurst, Max, Woodborough, Ford, Barton, Winscombe, Sidcot, Oakridge and Hale (Custumal of Winscombe, 1290). Although referring to the combined area of Winscombe, Ford and Woodborough today, the hamlet of Winscombe was formerly centred around the Church of St. James and the former Court house belonging to the Dean and Chapter of Wells.

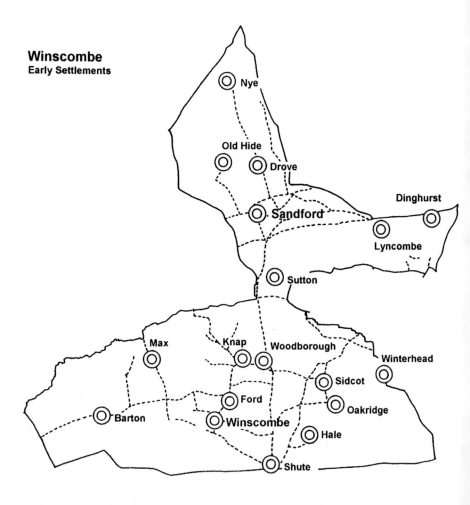

Winscombe
Early Settlements

Nye
Old Hide
Drove
Sandford
Dinghurst
Lyncombe
Sutton
Max
Knap
Woodborough
Winterhead
Sidcot
Ford
Oakridge
Barton
Winscombe
Hale
Shute

Winscombe Early Settlements by M A Aston

A WINSCOMBE HERMIT
by Professor Mick Aston

Thirty-two hermits are known to have existed in Somerset; approximately one third of these in the 14th and 15th centuries (Clay, 1914, 246; Dr Eddie Jones, pers. comm). One of these is Philip Shipham of St. Romanus, in Winscombe.

The only known documentary evidence for the Winscombe hermit occurs in Bishop Ralph's Register 1331 (Scott Holmes, 1895,70). It implies that the Bishop is granting a licence to a hermit in the parish and is asking people to help and support him.

"We ask and exhort you all in Christ, who are moreover firmly joined in the holy strength of fealty, on behalf of our beloved in Christ Philip Shipham who has established his poor hermitage in the parish of Winscombe in the place which is commonly called St. Romanus's. On account of that same dwelling, which as mentioned he began to construct, whoever, he (or his agents in his name carrying these letters), may approach among you and your faithful seeking alms, in the business of the said poor hermitage, kindly admit him to your churches or other places, so that he may lay out the business of the said poor hermitage to the clergy and people under subjection to you. We certainly wish that whatever will have been collected or gathered together on this account should be given to the said hermit or his agents. Finally we ..... to all our faithful in Christ in our diocese as an indulgence, who will give the said hermit support". Given at Banwell VII Ides of August AD 1331. (Translation Dr. Michael Costen).

There is documentary evidence for hermits in three main periods in Britain. During the 7th century sites were often eventually turned into abbey sites; there is evidence in the 12th century for groups of hermits; and in the 14th and 15th centuries, where there was not enough money for funding monasteries, chantry chapels were often financed or a holy man or hermit was approved and supported by the church.

The employment of hermits at this time was a manifestation of a general concern for personal salvation which can be seen elsewhere in the endowment of chantries with chantry priests and the popularity of the more spiritual and austere monastic and religious orders in the late Middle Ages. However, hermits needed to be licensed - that is given permission by the local Bishop - since there was much fear and concern by the Church about heresy and unorthodox beliefs. Hermits, when appearing before the Bishop, would have probably been bare-headed and barefoot and during the service the old garments would have been taken off and robes, suitable for a hermit, were blessed and then put on.

The hermit would have signed a deed and made a vow. An example of the type of oath taken by hermits can be found in the Register of Thomas Bekynton, Bishop of Bath and Wells 1443-1465 (Maxwell-Lyte and Dawes, 1934, 190). The Bishop immediately before celebrating mass in his chapel in the manor of Wookey, certified and approved the following profession made by John of Wells:

"I, John of Wells, not wedded promise and avow to God and Our Lady Saint Mary and to all the Saints of Heaven the full purpose, all perpetual chastity after the rule of Saint Paul the hermit in presence of your right reverend father in God Thomas, by the Grace of God, Bishop of Bath and Wells. In nomine Patris et Fillii et Spiritus Sancti, Amen".

John of Wells, who was unable to write, made his mark in the sign of the cross on the document and on receipt of this the Bishop presented him with a hermit's habit.

It is not known where the site of St. Romanus was in Winscombe: the place-name does not survive and it is not identifiable in earlier records. Suggested sites include: the cave at Wringstone (Barton) Rocks, woods along the Winscombe/Shipham boundary, adjacent to the several wells in the parish, or in the marshes to the north of Sandford. The hermitage could even have been in or near the church or churchyard although this seems unlikely given the reference to the "place" called St. Romanus.

A PLACE CALLED SAINT ROMANUS

by Frances Neale

There are a number of saints of this name, but the one with a particular Wells connection is Saint Romanus, Bishop of Rouen 630-639. Rouen was the principal cathedral of Normandy during the 1200's while it was still part of the English kingdom. English ecclesiastics spent much time in Normandy, either in attendance at the English Court which regularly toured the province, or when in exile from political/religious problems in England. Witness lists on charters suggest they were well acquainted with their opposite numbers in Normandy.

Bishop Jocelyn had been one of King John's closest advisors during the growth of troubles between the King and the Pope, which centred on who should choose the next Archbishop of Canterbury. In the end Bishop Jocelyn and his brother Hugh, then Bishop elect of Lincoln, went into exile, and the Pope excommunicated King John, closed churches and declared England under an Interdict until King John should cooperate.

Jocelyn and Hugh spent the years 1209-1213 in exile, mostly in Normandy and much of it in the vicinity of Rouen. Jocelyn returned to England and Wells in 1214 and work on building the new cathedral church resumed c.1220. Bishop Jocelyn dedicated the church of St. Andrew on the same day as he gifted the Manor of Winscombe to the Dean and Chapter of Wells. This date is recorded as St. Romanus Day, October 23rd, 1239 (Liber Albus I). Given Jocelyn's earlier association with the Rouen area, and Rouen's association with St. Romanus, still much in evidence in the cathedral and the city, it seems more than just chance that Jocelyn chose St. Romanus Day as the date to which to dedicate his new cathedral building.

It seems more than coincidence that just over one hundred years later, the hermit at Winscombe "has established his poor hermitage in the place which is commonly called St. Romanus's". No more is known about Philip Shipham, the hermit, and most tantalisingly, no recognisable place-name clue to the whereabouts of the place called St. Romanus's has so far been found.

THE FRATERNITY OF THE BLESSED VIRGIN

by Dr Joe Bettey

Documents from the late medieval period indicate that there was a Fraternity of the Blessed Virgin in Winscombe. The earliest reference is in the Somerset Chantries Surveys and Rentals (Green, 1888, 81-82) which mentions that the Fraternity possessed plate and ornament consisting of a chalice weighing nine ounces and Thomas Snarpon, aged forty years, was listed as the incumbent in the year 1548. Francis Knight (1915, 38) interprets these documents by suggesting that a monastic house had formerly existed in the parish and that it may have stood on the site which is now occupied by the Court even though he stated that no trace of anything of the nature of a monastic building remained and the site of it was unknown.

A study of the documents relating to this establishment by the author suggests that these entries do not refer to any monastic establishment, but to a guild or fraternity at Winscombe, with an altar or chapel within the parish church where a priest was endowed to say masses for members. Many such fraternities were established during the 14th and 15th centuries, and although we do not know precisely when the Winscombe Fraternity was founded, it no doubt dates from the period when the cult of the Blessed Virgin was at its height. The purpose of a fraternity was to offer an alternative for those who could not individually afford the expense of endowing a chantry chapel, such as the chantry chapel at Sandford. Members could join with others in financing a priest who would offer masses for the repose of their souls.

Evidence for the Fraternity being an integral part of the building of St. James is taken from a collection containing 16th century wills (Shilton and Holworthy, 1925). Various bequests were made to the parish church of Winscombe during that period. In 1543, William Saleway instructed that he was to be buried at St. James and included the bequest of "a cow the price of thirteen shillings and fourpence to the maintenance of Our Lady Service there". In the same year Thomas Davys alias Ruste of Winscombe died and was buried at St. James. In his will he bequeathed "a bushel of wheat to the church and high light" in addition to the sum of "three shillings and fourpence to the maintenance of our Lady service". In his will of 1544 John Gowed or Good of Winscombe instructed that ten shillings was to be given to "Our Lady's service at Wynscombe to be prayed for" as well as "half a bushel of barley to the high light". The chapel, maintained by the Fraternity, no doubt contained a statue of the Blessed Virgin before which the lights referred to would have been kept burning.

Although little is known about the foundation and functioning of the Fraternity, there is a great deal of information about its suppression. The Act for the Suppression of Chantries 1547 specifically included fraternities and by the Act all possessions were confiscated by the Crown.

During the next few years, the religious changes of the period would have meant that the statues, lights and ornaments, which had been maintained by the Fraternity in Winscombe parish church, would have been destroyed, along with the stone altars, wall paintings, screens and other relics of Catholic worship. Remarkably, some of the fine medieval stained glass in the Winscombe windows managed to survive this intense wave of destruction.

The sale of the chantry properties by the Crown resulted in an intense scramble among speculators anxious for a share of the spoils. The Crown Commissioner for Somerset, William Moryce, first surveyed the possessions of Winscombe Fraternity on 11th May 1548 (Woodward, 1982, 1-2). On 18th July 1548, a speculator named Robert Norton of Hallesworth in Suffolk bought the possessions of the former Fraternity at Winscombe as part of a larger purchase of such properties in various parts of the country (Cal Pat Rolls, 1547-8, 318-9).

On 18th December 1549, after long negotiation, Norton sold many of his Somerset purchases to George Payne, gentleman of Hutton, including lands and property in Winscombe and the chapel at Sandford.

In Hugo's Medieval Nunneries of the County of Somerset (1867, 206) the following entry is recorded: "On the 18th of December 1549, the King granted for £265.15s.6d to George Payne of Hutton in the County of Somerset, gentleman, the late Fraternity of the Blessed Virgin in Wynscombe with its lands". As a result of the slow working of the Court of Augmentations, which had been set up to oversee the sale of such property for the Crown, the royal licence confirming the sale to George Payne was finally granted on 13th May 1551.

According to Cardinal Pole's Pension Book of 1553, the last incumbent of the Fraternity, Thomas Snarpon, was retired and in receipt of a pension of four pounds a year (Green, 1888, 22).

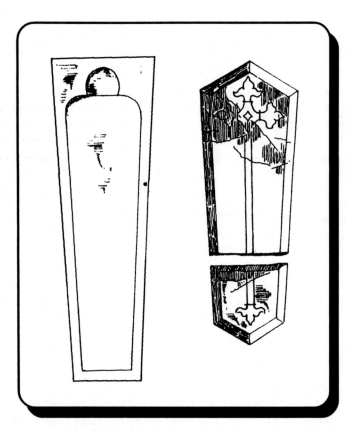

Coffin and 14th century slab at Winscombe Church
by R W Paul (1882)

THE CHURCH ON THE SIDE OF THE HILL

In Winscombe a new church was dedicated in 1236 to St. James the Great (HMC Wells, 1907, 361) and the first incumbent was William de Kaynesham (Liber Albus II). The font in the south aisle is probably one of the few visible remains of the 13th century church. The earliest documents concerning the 13th century church are held in the archives at Wells Cathedral. A board listing the incumbents of St. James is on the wall in the north aisle of the church (Appendix 1).

It has been suggested that Winscombe had a pre-13th century church (Aston, pers. comm). Prior to the 13th century the Manor of Winscombe was the possession of Glastonbury Abbey and it would have been highly likely that a church was built during their period of ownership. In the vast majority of parishes, church and clergy were already established by the mid 12th century and most had been founded by the 10th century. The position of the church is unusual as it is cut into a terrace on the side of a hill. One can only assume that it was already a significant site and this determined where the new church would be built. Perhaps the church was erected on the site of an earlier chapel, church or holy well, or the site may have been significant in pre-christian times (Aston, pers. comm).

There is reference to fragments of masonry discovered during the 19th century restoration of the church. Theodore Compton (1882, 45) interprets these as being part of a "Norman church" which had previously stood on the same site. Although Compton considers these remains to be "Norman", detailed architectural evidence is not presently available. Also during restoration of the church, workmen uncovered a stone coffin, near where the pulpit stands. The undated coffin, about six feet in length, is now situated in the churchyard on the south side of the tower. Beside the coffin is an incised cross slab of the late 14th century (Paul, 1882, 266). No one knows whose body it contained but presumably someone of importance.

THE PARISH CHURCH OF Sᵀ. JAMES, WINSCOMBE

by Maria Forbes

The 13th century church was dedicated to St. James the Great who was one of the twelve apostles. He was beheaded in about AD 44 and his relics became the focal point of pilgrimage in Santiago de Compostela during the 12th century. It has been suggested that this type of dedication is usually associated with churches of that period. This may give support to the theory that the 13th century church was a replacement for an earlier church and was a re-dedication to St. James (Aston and Neale, pers. comm).

A statue of St. James the Great can be seen in a niche on the outside of the 15th century tower above the nave. He is dressed as a pilgrim and looking towards the east. St. James is usually identified by the symbols associated with him: a cockle shell, a water bottle, and a pilgrim's hat and staff.

The exact date of reconstruction of the existing church is unknown but it is of Perpendicular style (15th century). At that time the Dean and Chapter were investing profits from Mendip sheep farming in their churches. The earliest illustration of the church at Winscombe appears on Bishop Hobhouse's Map of the Commons of Mendip which dates from the 16th century. While this has some inaccuracies, the tower is correctly placed and the decorated parapet is accurately represented. Documents provide further information about the fabric of the church. On 30th July 1610 it was reported that the chancel of the church was set on fire by negligence or oversight and it was ordered that the roof be repaired and covered with hard tile (HMC Wells, 1907, 359).

PETER CARSLEIGH,
A LATE-MEDIEVAL VICAR OF WINSCOMBE

Peter Carsleigh was born in Lustleigh, Devon c.1454 and had a long association with the Dean and Chapter of Wells and its benefices (Woodforde, 1946, 149-154). In 1483 he became a student at Exeter College, Oxford where he took degrees of Master of Arts and Doctor of Divinity. In 1493 he was admitted as a canon of Wells Cathedral and about three years later he was appointed vicar of Broadclyst in Devon. In 1501 Peter Carsleigh was named as one of the two keepers of the cathedral library and in 1503 he was appointed steward of the cathedral. From 1513-1517 he held the rich and important vicarage of Menheniot in Cornwall.

On 5th March 1521, on the death of John Vele, Peter Carsleigh was appointed vicar of Winscombe. However he already had an association with the parish of Winscombe. On 16th May 1509 Peter Carsleigh took possession of a close annexed to the house of the Manor of Winscombe and a piece of underwood for fifty years, paying fifteen shillings per annum, with the condition that he should turn the underwood into pasture as soon as possible (HMC Wells, 1914, 213).

Peter Carsleigh held the living of Winscombe until his resignation in 1532 although there is confusion in Knight (1915, 44) concerning the dates of his incumbency. At the age of nearly 80 Peter mistakenly prayed in public for Queen Catherine of Aragon in Wells Cathedral instead of Queen Anne Boleyn, the current wife of King Henry VIII. This mistake was reported to Thomas Cromwell by the Bishop in some detail (Woodforde, 1946,151). Peter Carsleigh died soon after. His will dated 5th August 1534 was proved 21st January 1535.

One of the oldest existing windows in Winscombe church has a link with Peter Carsleigh. The north window of the chancel bears an incomplete inscription which would suggest that Peter Carsleigh had the window made during the early part of the 16th century (Woodforde, 1946, 153). The three figures in the window are: in the middle light, St. Peter the Apostle; on the left St. Peter the Deacon; and on the right, St. Peter the Exorcist. It would seem that the window was especially made to incorporate his three name-saints.

16th century Carsleigh Window in north wall of chancel

THE PARISH AND THE POOR

P A system to take care of those suffering hardship was the responsibility of the parish. Relief was given to supplement income and was raised from levies on land owners and parishioners. A complete list of the people paying the Poor Rate was made in addition to an account of how the money was distributed. In Winscombe these registers date from 1679 (S.R.O. D/P/Winsc 13) and at that time the Poor Rate was set at twelve pence in the pound. Pauper burials and christenings are marked in the parish registers with a 'P'.

Regular payments of a few shillings were made, sometimes over a long period, to villagers in illness or in distress. Items of warm clothing, bedding and shoes were purchased for their benefit. Sums of money were also paid for the purchase of alcohol in illness: 2s.0d for a pint of rum or brandy and 1s.0d for a pint of gin! A doctor was appointed to look after the sick. In 1757 an entry in the Vestry Minutes (D/P/Winsc 9) details the agreement made between the church officials and James Rich, a surgeon of Axbridge. He was to be paid five guineas per annum "for taking care and administering phisick to all the poor of the parish and that if any person was afflicted in any extraordinary manner then they would be sent to the Bristol Infirmary".

Many regular payments from Poor Rate funds were made to the poor, especially in the winter months. Sacks of coal at 1s.7d a sack were bought for individual households. Coal at 13s.0d a load was purchased and distributed in December 1791: one for the poor at Sidcot, one for the poor at Sandford and one for the Poor House.

The burial of the poor was also the responsibility of a parish and in 1704, several payments were made when Thomas Clege died including: 4s.6d for a coffin, 2s.6d to Samuel Hooper, for making the grave and ringing the bell and 11d for a loaf and 2s.1d for a cheese "for the burying".

Personal bequests were also made for the benefit of the poor of the parish. When Francis Taylor Doolan died in 1842 (Knight, 1915, 55), he left the sum of two hundred and fifty pounds invested in the West Harptree Turnpike Trust. The interest was to be used to provide warm clothing to the aged and infirm of the parish with preference being given to those who attend the Protestant church and no other. Unfortunately, this investment proved to be an unwise one producing very little interest. In his will he also stated that "my ancestors were for many generations gentlemen, and several of them vicars of the parish of Winscombe ....".

Only those who were permanently resident in a parish were entitled to financial relief. New arrivals were only allowed to settle in the parish providing they had a certificate from their home parish guaranteeing to take them back if they required financial support. In 1714 a payment of 2s.6d was made by the Overseers of Winscombe "to a poor woman, being big with child, to send her out of the parish". Payments of a few pence were made to poor men and women "on the road".

CHURCH BUILDINGS

The Parsonage House

An early reference to "the house of the Manor of Winscombe" (HMC Wells, 1914, 213) may refer to the dwelling that became known as the Parsonage House of Winscombe. The close held by Peter Carsleigh in 1509 was annexed to "the house of the Manor of Winscombe". Later Dean and Chapter documents refer to "the orchard that one Peter Caseley sometime held, parcel of the said Parsonage" (Stewards Proposals Wells, 1674, 68).

To date the first known mention of the Parsonage is in a 1613 Glebe Terrier of Winscombe (DD/OB 39). The house was leased to Mr George Roynon providing additional income for the Dean and Chapter of Wells. However manorial business was still carried out at the house. A condition to the Parsonage lease is described in a 1650 Parliamentary Survey of the Manor of Winscombe (DD/CC 110733) as: "The Lessee for himself his heirs and assignes, covenant during the term aforesaid, once every year upon due warning given to prepare and find convenient meat, drink and lodging for the steward of the said Dean and Chapter and his company, and also horse meal, litter, provender and stable room for their horses, by the space of two days and one night at The Parsonage House in Winscombe aforesaid and shall suffer and permit the lessors and their steward to keep Courts at the accustomed place there" (transcribed by Maria Forbes).

Additionally in 1650 under the same Act of Parliament, a separate survey of the Parsonage or Rectory of Winscombe (DD/OB 33) was carried out which included a very detailed description of the dwelling and its associated outbuildings. The Parsonage house and outbuildings covered an area of three acres. The house contained a hall, a parlour, a kitchen, a buttery and seven chambers. Associated with the house were a brewhouse, a dairy house, a stable, other outhouses, three gardens, two orchards, one court-yard with other little yards, one large barn, one stall, one "wain house", one dovehouse, one small hop yard and "one more barton" [farm yard].

The first map evidence for a Parsonage or Rectory is taken from the 1792 William White map of Winscombe (DD/CC 10762). The building now occupying this site is Winscombe Court.

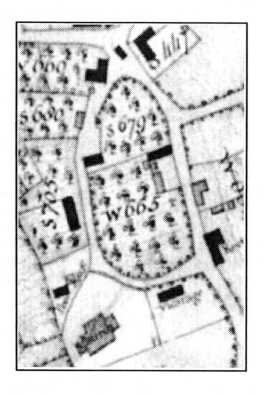

Detail from William White map of Winscombe, 1792

The Vicarage

In the Glebe Terrier there is also concurrent documentary evidence for both a Vicarage and a Parsonage house in Winscombe in 1613. At that time there was a dwelling house belonging to the Vicar, with a garden and orchard which was bounded on the south "by the hill or waste" and on the north by a piece of ground called The Cutthayes. This document also lists details of tithes due to the vicar (DD/OB 39).

As for the Parsonage, the first map evidence for the Vicarage is taken from the 1792 William White map of Winscombe (DD/CC 10762). Francis Knight (1915, 37) briefly mentions that the original vicarage site was occupied by two cottages. This site is currently occupied by the church car park. The building now referred to as the Old Vicarage is shown on the 1840 Tithe Map and Award for Winscombe (DD/CTN 130, 131) and was occupied by Reverend C. Cobley. However, this house is situated further south than the original building which suggests that it had been re-sited. Further evidence is found in the Particulars and Conditions of Sale of Winscombe Vicarage (1963) which states a construction date of 1836 for this building.

While it was not necessary for the Vicar of Winscombe to be a resident, in the 18th century at least, it was a condition that the curate should reside within the parish. Evidence is taken from the parish Vestry Minute Book of 1746 (D/P/winsc/9): " It is agreed that whatever person shall succeed the Reverend Mr John Taylor, the present curate of this parish, that he the said curate do reside within the said parish..." Reverend John Taylor, died in 1781 and at the age of 72. He was buried inside the communion rails close to the right hand wall. In the parish register he was described as: "A man truly beloved by all the country and dearly missed by all the surrounding parishes as a friend to all denominations of man. He studied the happiness of the rich and courted the esteem of the poor in general".

The Church House

Over a long period of time parish churches were not only the focus for religious life but also social events. Buildings known as church houses were especially constructed for social gatherings. Early in the 18th century Winscombe still had a church house somewhere in the vicinity of the churchyard, and in 1704 payments were made to repair its thatched roof (Knight, 1915, 49).

The Poor House

Evidence for the Poor House in Winscombe is taken from two sources. On the 1792 estate map two buildings to the north-west of the churchyard are designated as the Poor House. Francis Knight (1915, 51) also refers to the original Poor House as consisting of two small cottages on the north-west side of the churchyard separated by a wall from the church itself.

The date of construction is not known but documents suggest it was already in existence by 1713. In that year a young man was paid 8d for going on errands concerning the Poor House. By the 1790s more information is available about its structure (D/P/Winsc 13). In March 1792 it would seem that more major repairs were carried out as £1.7s.5½d was paid out when the thatch of the Poor House was repaired and 19s.5½d was paid for timber and to carpenters in respect of the same. One week later, 2d was paid to lime the building. Every item of expenditure for the Poor House was listed. In 1791, a total of 6s.0d was spent on the purchase of a frying pan, a lock and the cost of having the chimney swept.

In 1799 negotiations started to move the Poor House to Woodborough (DD/CC c/2208). The leaseholder of The Parsonage, Francis Edwards Whalley: "gave to George Phippen, Church Warden, and Arthur Hancock, Overseer of the Poor of the parish of Winscombe, part of

Woodborough Green and the house lately built thereon in exchange for the messuage or dwelling house and garden now occupied by the poor of the said parish of Winscombe bounded on the east by the highway leading to Winscombe church on the south by the church yard and on the north and west by old enclosures". Knight (1915, 51) records that "many decades before" the occupier of Winscombe Court had objected to the proximity of the paupers to his residence and had given the parish a plot of land containing a row of cottages on Woodborough Green for a new Poor House. These cottages provided a total of fourteen rooms.

One can only assume from this that the person objecting to the proximity of the paupers was in fact Mr Whalley. The position of the Poor House next to the church and the proposed Poor House on Woodborough Green are clearly marked on the Enclosure Award maps (DD/CC c/2208).

In 1838 the families of the poor of the parish were given notice by the Churchwardens of Winscombe that they had to leave the Poor House as they were to be re-housed in the newly-built Union Workhouse at Axbridge. Obviously the tenants did not go willingly. They were reluctant to leave their rural home to move to the Workhouse, and the authorities had difficulty in removing them (Knight, 1915, 51).

Next to the church, the cottages which had formerly housed the poor of the parish were apparently still standing until the middle of the 19th century when they were pulled down. The site was once more included in the area of the churchyard and the dividing wall was buried. From the detail shown on the Enclosure Map, it would seem that the former Poor House on Woodborough Green now consists of several cottages, called South View and includes one known as Old Alms Cottage.

CHURCHWARDENS

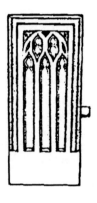 Normally two Churchwardens are appointed and they represent the whole parish, not merely the members of the Church of England (Dale, 1957, 29). Churchwardens were formerly responsible for many aspects of their parish. This included the allocation of pews and provision of facilities for worship. It was not until the later medieval period that pews were introduced into the naves of churches as parishioners had formerly stood or knelt during services. After the introduction of seating, the Churchwardens subsequently charged people for the right to sit in the pews (D/P/Winsc 9). George Symons was given permission in 1807 to divide his pew at his own expense, retaining the western part for his own use. At the same time, William Downs Phillott was granted full liberty to erect a pew under the gallery for his own use.

In 1783 a rate of sixpence in the pound was payable to Winscombe towards the necessary repairs of the church. On 12th November, 1783 2s.6d was paid "for raising gravel on Heverendown to make a church path to the chancel door". Heverendown is one of the ancient names for Wavering Down.

Also included in the Churchwardens' duties were the supervision of the education and relief of the poor, the maintenance of parish arms and the payment of local soldiers, and the control of vermin. In 1704, John Burges was paid 3s.4d for killing ten polecats.

Today their duties include: the collection of alms, the disposal of the communion alms, the allocation of seats, the parochial registers and the protection of church property.

VICARS AND THE 19th CENTURY RESTORATION OF THE CHURCH

During the 19th century the Anglican church became revitalised in all respects. In the first half of the century the population of England and Wales doubled and many new churches were built in order to accommodate the growing population. There were also many churches in urgent need of repair throughout the country at this time, including the church at Winscombe.

Charles Cobley - Vicar of Winscombe 1828-1859

Charles James Cobley was born in 1790, the son of Reverend John Cobley, vicar of Cheddar and his wife Elizabeth. Charles was ordained in 1816. At the age of 38 Charles became the Vicar of Winscombe. In the 1841 Census, Charles was residing at the Vicarage with John his brother and two female servants; Hannah Corner and Harriet Reeves. In the 1851 Census, Charles and John were listed as unmarried and aged 61 and 68 respectively. When Hannah Corner died in 1853, a memorial stone was erected in the churchyard to the south of the chancel by Charles Cobley which bears the inscription, " She was a truly faithful servant for 42 years. She died much regretted".

Charles Cobley became the first to commence the long process of the repair of the parish church in the 19th century. Early in the 19th century the church music was of a "rustic kind" until modernised (Compton, 1892, 58). The singing was led and supported by a village choir and a band consisting of two "clarionets, a bassoon and a serpent". Charles Cobley gave a "seraphine" to the church which took the place of these former musicians. In 1850 he also financed work on the crucifixion window in the Lady Chapel.

Charles Cobley was Vicar of Winscombe until his death in 1859 at the age of 69 and additional information concerning his private life in Winscombe can be taken from his will (D/PWinsc 18/1/1). Charles was in receipt of income from freehold land and property outside the parish. On Charles' death provision was made to provide a residence in the neighbourhood of Winscombe for his brother, John, as "he had become accustomed to take drives in his carriage" but unfortunately no suitable residence was found. Charles stated that he had resided with his brother in the Vicarage House for more than twenty years and that "John was, and always had been, of weak mind and was in need of much personal care and attention". A memorial tablet to the whole Cobley family is on the wall in the north aisle which includes details of the death of John Cobley in 1866 "who was the last surviving member of the family". Charles and John are buried in the churchyard to the south of the chancel, next to their servant Hannah.

Winscombe Church, 1836 by John Buckler

William Harkness - Vicar of Winscombe 1859-1863

William Harkness was born in Middlesex and became a student at Eton and then Cambridge University. He was listed as a rowing "Blue" in 1845. He was ordained in 1848, in 1853 he married Sarah Anne and in 1859 William became the Vicar of Winscombe. In the 1861 Census, William Harkness (37 years of age) and his wife Sarah Anne (36) were living at the Vicarage together with their children: William (7), Jane (5), Grace (4), and Maude (1). There were also six female servants including a governess, cook, nurse and domestic servants.

William Harkness raised the majority of the money required for the church restoration (Compton, 1892, 59) and he personally contributed £100 towards the repair of the chancel. This restoration work was completed in 1864 using a donation of £500 from Reverend John Yatman, a gentleman-cleric residing at Winscombe Hall (Compton, 1882, 47) and a painted window was inserted in memory of his mother, Ellen Yatman, who had died in 1858. The Yatman family were patrons of William Burges, the Victorian architect, and they commissioned him to design a new triple lancet window in the east end of the chancel. This window is often wrongly accredited to William Morris (Crook, 1981, 224). Some of the medieval tracery of the former window was installed in 1875 in West Lodge, Winscombe Hill which was owned by John Yatman.

Through the efforts of William Harkness, Winscombe gained its first small church organ and the choir standards were improved. The choir was formerly seated in a gallery in the lower storey of the tower. Evidence for a singer's gallery is found in the Vestry Minutes Book of 1747 (D/P/Winsc.9/1/1) which mentions the building of such a gallery by Edward Edny who was paid twenty-two guineas. During the 1863 restoration (Dodd, 1924), the gallery was removed and the space was opened up to the vaulted roof. At the same time the bell ringers' entrance within the tower was blocked up and a new exterior entrance was made. For the first time, the choristers became surpliced as a result of being more conspicuously seated in the area of the chancel which was no

Early 20th century photograph of Winscombe Church
after the restoration of the chancel

longer blocked off by a screen (Compton, 1892, 59). It was also considered more appropriate that the choristers were suitably attired during the newly-introduced procession of clergy and choir.

William Harkness died in 1863 at Ventnor, Isle of Wight, at the age of 39, just before the restoration work had been completed. A memorial tablet on the wall of the north aisle was erected with the following inscription: "With untiring energy and warm affection, he devoted his strength, his time, his means, to promote among the parishioners the saving knowledge of the Lord, Christ Jesus. His brief career was earnest service in the Redeemer's cause. How truly he was loved, how deeply mourned. This tablet is erected to record - well done good and faithful Servant, enter thou into the joy of the Lord."

The Follett Family and the Church of St. James

Richard Follett was born in Taunton in 1828 the son of the Reverend Richard Francis Follett, Head Master of Taunton Collegiate School. Richard later became a student of St. John's College, Cambridge and also Wells Theological College. He was ordained in 1858 and served as a curate in Devon and Somerset before being appointed Vicar of Winscombe in 1863. During his incumbency the restoration work begun by Charles Cobley and William Harkness was completed.

According to the 1871 Census, Reverend Richard Follett was 42 years old and still unmarried. His sister Caroline Follett was living with him at the Vicarage with three domestic servants. Later in the year Richard married Mary Ann Rawlison, 22 years old, daughter of George Rawlison. Her residence at that time was listed as Winscombe Hill. It is possible that this is the same person who was listed in the 1871 Census as Mary A Rawling 22, a governess to the Yatman children at The Hall. By 1886 Richard and Mary Follett had three sons and seven daughters: Ethel Mary, Annie Dora, Montague Beadon, Francis Bere, William Carrington, Jessie Margaret, Mary Dawbney, Dorothy Anne, Cicely Helen and Sybilla Alice. On 27th December 1878, the third son, William Carrington Follett, died at the age of fourteen months.

Richard Follett retired as Vicar of Winscombe in 1895 at the age of 67 and he and his family joined his sister Mrs Lethbridge at Winscombe Court. Fanny Lethbridge (née Follett), was the widow of Ambrose Goddard Lethbridge. Ambrose and Fanny had no children and by 1881, according to the Census, Fanny now widowed, had moved to Winscombe Court which occupied the site of the previous Parsonage House. From 1867 to 1880 there are no references in either the Census or Directories to Winscombe Court. It would seem that the former Parsonage House had been demolished during this period.

One of the windows in the north aisle is a memorial to Montague Beadon Follett, the eldest son of Richard and Mary Follett who died on 7th July 1900 during the Boer War, at the age of 25. He had gone to South Africa as a volunteer in the Ceylon Contingent and died of enteric fever.

The Follett Family (1894)   *(Back row from left) Dora, Francis,Ethel*
(middle row) Jessie, Richard, Mary, Montague, May
(Front row) Dorothy, Sybilla? Cicely?

Jessie Margaret, daughter of Reverend Richard Follett, retained her contacts with Winscombe until her death. She was born in the Vicarage in 1879. In 1901 she married Herman Alexander Tiarks in Winscombe Church, an event described in great detail by the local press. The church was lavishly decorated with flowers and after a reception held at Winscombe Court, the newly-married couple travelled to the village railway station, passing through an arch of flowers which had been erected over the main entrance. Many villagers had also decorated their houses with flowers and "goodwill" messages. "Detonators" had also been placed along the railway line"! In 1908 Webbington House was built for Herman Tiarks and Jessie was responsible for creating the ornamental gardens there (Jordan, 1994, 79). Jessie died from tuberculosis in 1923 at the age of 45 in a Swiss sanatorium. Her body was brought back to her place of birth and she is buried in the south-east corner of Winscombe Churchyard close to the boundary wall. Herman did not re-marry and in 1955 he was buried with Jessie. Many other members of the Follett family are also buried in this area of the churchyard.

Richard Follett, of Winscombe Court, died in 1907 aged 79 and was described in a newspaper obituary as "an absolutely ideal country cleric, a genial, kind hearted man approachable by all who took the deepest interests in any good movement connected with his own parish or the surrounding district". On the day of his funeral the minute bell at Winscombe Church tolled and the Ensign was lowered to half-mast. The polished elm coffin, with its black furniture, was carried by four bearers; the sexton and three "workmen" from Winscombe Court. Later in 1907, permission was granted to erect a reredos of carved Caen stone in the chancel at Winscombe Church, the subject to be "The Ascension of Our Lord". This reredos was commissioned by Mrs Lethbridge of Winscombe Court in memory of her brother, Richard.

A Follett Memorial Fund was also set up by the parishioners in order to raise money for the chancel seats. Many villagers contributed to the fund and in 1909 the seating was installed at a cost of £87.17s.0d. The seating was dedicated to the memory of Reverend Richard Follett on 23rd April 1909 by the Archdeacon of Wells. Four additional windows in the church are also dedicated to various members of the Follett family.

Winscombe Church decorated for Easter, 1894

Winscombe Vicarage (1894)

Winscombe Court (1894)

PILGRIM'S REGRESS

by Reverend Bernard Salmon

A Sermon preached in 1986 in
Winscombe Parish Church
at the start of the
750th ANNIVERSARY YEAR

"Come back with me one hundred years, to 1886....

St. James' church looked very much the same then as it does now. The most noticeable change would be that they had not got electric lighting and we have more space to move about. The great Restoration some twenty years before had resulted in as many seats as could be fitted in - because they needed those seats for the people who wanted to come to church. That this made possible a sizeable income from pew-rents was quite secondary: though all the important families had their own seats (and used them every week). There was a feeling of stability about society. The Church was respected, even though the tithe was burdensome, and non-conformists resented the Church's imagined privileges. They also criticised the latest fashions in church furnishings, which they were sure would lead the Church of England into the arms of Rome.

Their latest foible was to have an organ and a robed choir. The Singing Gallery at the west end had just been taken down, and there were the singers, as bold as brass, sitting on either side of the chancel. Still, what could one expect with all these new-fangled hymns to be learned? They weren't in the Prayer Book, hymns weren't: what was wrong with the Psalms?

Hymns had made their mark a hundred years before, and if we go back to 1786 we find that John and Charles Wesley (who had been responsible for many of them) were still alive. They were regarded as disturbers of the status quo, with their singing and preaching and enthusiasm. The French Revolution in a year or two's time would prove even more of a disturbance. But the Church of England in these parts wasn't duly affected, even if the miners in neighbouring Shipham were.

Not many people actually lived in Winscombe valley anyhow, perhaps a few hundred all told, and those that did were far too busy scratching a living, all except the gentry of course, to concern themselves with new-fangled ideas. In towns it might be different. And where there was water-power the new industrial revolution was beginning to make itself felt. But nothing, it seemed, had changed in Winscombe for centuries. They made do with what they had.

Fortunately, the church was reasonably sound. The roof leaked, of course, and the floor was damp, and uneven, and there was no heating. Still, since the building was only used on a Sunday it didn't seem of great importance. But no wonder it smelt musty, and there was a general air of neglect.

The pews had rotted in places, but they had been patched up. The old Rood Screen at the entrance of the chancel had become rickety, and they had taken it down, as it seemed pointless to repair what served no useful purpose. The old glass had been made waterproof, but a lot was missing. The best thing in the church was its bells, newly put in a few years before. They rang those with gusto at festivals.

Although they hadn't much money for repairs, parishioners were fond of their church. They brought their babes for Baptism, and laid their coffins on the fine new bier at funeral times. Some of the well-to-do remembered the church in their wills: like Jane Wheeler, widow of a canon of Wells, who in 1772 gave a Communion Flagon (which we still use regularly), or Sarah Sherwood, the pair of Patens and Chalices in 1784 (which we do not).

Parson got along somehow in the cottage which was his vicarage; he visited them in their homes, and they wrapped up warm when they came to Morning or Evening Prayer to hear him read one of the Homilies For the rest of the time they left church affairs to him and the Churchwardens, who looked after a rough-and-ready welfare service, and what we would call local government. But the 1700's were not times when the Church of England exactly flourished.

What was it like a century before, in 1686?

As far as the church was concerned, the most obvious difference would be the great wooden screen right across the chancel arch and aisles.

Beyond it stood the Communion Table, with benches all round for the quarterly service of the Lord's Supper. Otherwise the services were all in the nave, and the big three-decker pulpit, reading desk, and clerk's pew stood at the head of it.

The upheavals of the Civil War had not come much nearer than Bristol. Nor had Monmouth's Rebellion: though a few hotheads from Winscombe had been attracted to it. People talked about King James II's preferences for the Roman Catholic faith, but matters had not come to a head in 1686. The Church of England was much more interested in having shaken itself loose from the oppressive puritan rule of Cromwell's Roundheads, and was revelling in its freedom; freedom to use again its Book of Common Prayer, and to celebrate the festivals of the Christian Year, and to enjoy the jollifications frowned on after the Civil War. Its Clergy were back again from exile, and people started to value the Anglican tradition of being both catholic and reformed, in a way they had not until they had almost lost it. The only casualty of the Commonwealth seems to have been the Parish Registers: they had to open a new Register at the Restoration, before which there are no records.

Fortunately Winscombe church had been too far off the beaten track to have its carvings defaced, or its windows smashed as idolatrous. Elsewhere more destruction had been wrought during Cromwell's dictatorship (and all in the name of religion) than at any time in the Church's history, except at the hands of well-intentioned Victorian restorers. But these harsh experiences hardened people's attitudes. The Restoration of the Monarchy under Charles II was accompanied by coercive legislation, such as the Act of Uniformity, with only limited concessions to the Puritans. But at least dissent no longer carried a sentence of being burnt at the stake: dissidents were to spend long terms in prison instead, as John Bunyan knew well (and turned to good account) - he was nearing the end of his life in 1686.

Back we go again, another century, to 1586.

Elizabeth I ruled then, though under threat from Spain. The Armada arrived in 1588, and Winscombe would have seen the beacons on the surrounding hills that fateful year. But in 1588 church affairs were still settling down to the new order of things which Elizabeth and her advisors were encouraging. They tried to combine as much of the

Catholic tradition on the one hand, with its sacramental observances and externals like vestments and set liturgical forms, and on the other the Protestant theology based on the Bible not the Pope, as the source of authority. This she did largely from political astuteness, seeing that the loyalties of most of her subjects were to the faith in which they had been brought up, while at the same time most of her power depended on the new families who had a vested interest in the Reformation Settlement. They held the Abbey lands, and did not want to give them up.

The Abbeys and Monasteries no longer controlled half the land of England. An elected Parliament was flexing its political muscles. Throughout Europe independence was all the rage: for Christendom under Emperor and Pope as colleagues was now giving way to a series of nations, each under its Prince.

Many new ideas were showing themselves even in the parish church of Winscombe. The walls were whitewashed to obliterate the painted pictures. The attire of the Vicar was somewhat simpler, for although chasuble and cope were still required by law, surplice and stole or scarf sufficed. The services were in English not Latin, but were still recognisably the same services. The old landmarks were still there. There were still candles on the altar, but not so many. The statues had been hidden away. The figure of Christ on the Cross, flanked by Mary and John, which had dominated the church from the Rood Screen, had gone - but it was still there in the stained glass. The Angelus still chimed at midday, and festivals and fasts continued as before.

The two main differences were that the vicar was now married - which scandalised some! and Masses were no longer paid to be said for the souls of the departed (which had been an imposition anyhow). But having no income from these chantries meant that in some places there was not sufficient money to pay for a chantry priest, who doubled as schoolmaster, so that schooling suffered. Superstition was discouraged at the cost of greater ignorance: that was just one of the anomalies. But Elizabethan England was aware of belonging to a new age of openness and enterprise: great things lay ahead...

But we are heading in the other direction. Back to 1486. And that really is to cross a watershed in the life of the parish church (and England too).

For the 1480's saw the end of the Middle Ages. The New Learning had been spreading in its influence for a while, though England had scarcely awakened to the changes in store. Politically the Tudors had to still establish their new era in place of the Plantagenets.

Economically Henry's nouveau riche followers had to lay hold on the sources of power. At the start of that century it had been the Church making the running. (It had been the Dean and Chapter of Wells for instance who had paid for the fine new nave and tower at Winscombe, out of their profits from wool). At the end of it, it would be the merchant guilds and private lay entrepreneurs who would be lavishing their benefactions on chantries and schools and churches.

England in 1486 saw Caxton printing books - but most were still in Latin (though Germany had had a Bible in German twenty years before: things were stirring there). England was behind the times. But at least she was spared the latest repressions, as in Spain, where Torquemada's Inquisition was tightening the screw on revival.

The Parish Church of Saint James the Great in Winscombe was still at the peak of its medieval splendour. Its new stonework and fine nave in the latest Perpendicular style provided plenty of space for the community. They were only just thinking of putting in fixed seats. Normally the floor was open and rush-strewn, an ideal place for meetings and markets and parties, with the dim chancel beyond its locked screen as an ever-present reminder of God's presence. But even the dim chancel was transformed: for the patrons had just replaced the narrow lancets of its east window with a great open Perpendicular window of many lights, to match those in the nave - and benefactors had filled them with the latest stained glass.

The parishioners of Winscombe thought highly of their church, preferring it to those of Banwell and Cheddar which had just been completed too, though both were already planning to raise their nave roofs to give a loftier appearance. Winscombe in 1486 was well content (even though for some reason they had just got through three vicars in as many years).

But we have nowhere like penetrated far enough back to reach the original church whose Consecration we have been celebrating this week. There are still two hundred and fifty years to go!

Let's take that in two stages: first back to 1386.

Chaucer was just starting his Canterbury Tales in 1386. Less than a generation ago the Black Death had swept the country, and the decimated population was still jangled, and struggling to survive. The Monasteries were still powerful - none more so than Glastonbury, who had been the patron when the church at Winscombe had been built. Now it was one hundred and fifty years old.

It had lasted well, though it was a bit small for the population, even allowing for the ravages of the plague. Its narrow windows - a throwback to an earlier age - made it very dark inside. But that didn't matter, as no one but the priest at the altar had a book to read from, and he had plenty of candles to help him see. The atmosphere was pretty thick too, what with the incense, and the burnt sheeps-tallow of the candles. But it smelt cosy, which was some compensation for the chill. And the colourful ritual gave solace to the villagers who in their piety crowded in to say their private prayers, and tell their beads, and support the priest in saying Mass for the living and the dead - even though they didn't understand a word of it: and sometimes the priest wasn't much more certain.

The hamlet of Winscombe, high up on the hillside above the swampy meadows was proud to provide the parish church for the whole secluded valley that lay spread out below with its scattered farms. They only had to look up to be reminded that God was there in their midst.

One final step back a century-and-a-half takes us to 1236....

The year of the completion of the first little Early English church here. What is left of it now is incorporated in our present chancel, and it was just about the same size. William de Kaynesham had been Vicar of Winscombe for ten years. He had been sent by his great Abbey of Keynsham to this backwater to rally the villagers in support of the Bishop's project to have churches built for each community. At last he had fulfilled his brief. He had managed to extract the resources needed (mostly in kind, for money was hard to come by). One had given timber, another stone, others had offered their oxen for carting it. The Bishop provided masons - though he wasn't keen to see them leave the work of adding the great west front to the Minster Church of St. Andrew at Wells

And now the carpenters had swept up the final shavings from the floor, and villages had scattered sweet herbs as a covering for the flagstones. There was a stout iron-studded door - two, actually: one for himself, and the other at the west end for the people. The latter entered directly into the dark little church. At least, nowadays we would call it small: but then it was the largest stone-built building in the village, except for the great barn, which belonged to the Bishop. And it was dark because window-glass was expensive, and so instead the wind-eyes had wooden shutters across them. There were three lancets on each side, and three grouped together over the Altar. But there were rush-lights along the walls, and six fine beeswax candles on prickets on the Altar - the gift of the old Abbot of Keynsham, who had been present with Bishop Jocelin for the Consecration last week.

The glory of that Consecration service was still fresh in William's mind. Some of the fine vestments had gone: the jewelled processional cross had been borrowed: but there was still enough finery to do honour to God and his Saints (particularly to Saint James, patron saint of this new parish, a reminder of pilgrimage and of progress to come).

William remembered how the Bishop and his acolytes had gone all round the church, first outside and then in, sprinkling holy water to claim the site for God, and to exclude all evil influences. The Bishop had marked seven consecration crosses on the walls, and paused to bless the west door, and the massive stone font just inside, and his prayer desk. Then he had solemnly marked out a great cross with the butt of his crozier in the fresh river sand sprinkled on the paving before the Altar, to hallow and consecrate this building for all time. Finally there had been a tiny relic to enclose in the stone Altar-slab, and only then could the Bishop and his Clerks celebrate High Mass, and bring the new church into use for the Worship of Almighty God.

William de Kaynesham thought well of Bishop Jocelin Trotman, a local man, brought up in Wells. He might live in Bath, but it was rumoured that he would like to return to Wells, and that his dignifying of the great church of St. Andrew there was a sign that he would like to make it his cathedral church. He was a great builder.

It had been a privilege to have Bishop Jocelin come over from his summer palace at Banwell to consecrate this new church in Winscombe.

William felt he was living in stirring times, with so much evidence of new life in the Church. He wondered how future generations would look back on the humble beginnings he had made, and whether this little building would survive to tell the tale of devotion and high hopes in that era of Magna Carta ....

Someone else also remembered the Consecration Day - and did so in practical fashion by making a gift to the Church to mark the occasion. Moreover, he made sure of recording the date of his gift, which is how we know it took place on 26th August 1236. All the official records have perished: but Henry Luveseft's Deed of Gift survives. This was the day this local farmer endowed his church with the gift of ploughland, a meadow, and an aldergrove called 'Durnhete', which probably lay in the valley bottom, towards Max Mills. We have reason to be grateful to him not just for his generosity, but for enabling us to be precise in celebrating the 750th year of the Consecration of our Parish Church.

William and Jocelin, Henry and many others who have loved this church, are with us still as fellow-worshippers: part of the host of angels and archangels and all the company of heaven - unseen, but present still in spirit. We are custodians now of this building which meant so much to them: and custodians also of the good news of our Living Lord Jesus which is why it still means so much to you and me. For it was built in his honour - God's house, where he meets us still, and from which we go out to tell and to show others how much the Faith of Christ means to us in the Twentieth Century.

At no time is the Church more than 'one generation thick'. In theory it could die out if a single generation failed to pass on what it had inherited and found to be true. That is why it matters so much that we should be faithful too".

INCUMBENTS OF THE PARISH CHURCH
ST JAMES, WINSCOMBE

	William de Kaynesham	1611	Matthew Woolf
	Walter de Cusington	1645	Robert Dayer
1241	John de Kaynesham	1662	John Smith
1256	Thomas Corbyn	1669	William Stuckey
1282	William de la Nye	1670	William Crofts
	Robert de Codeford	1671	William Olderson
1315	Robert de Lee	1678	Thomas Randolph
1316	Thomas de Schawebury	1697	Francis Taylor
1338	John de Pody	1736	John Woodford
1348	John Horn	1746	Samuel Squire
	Richard Wyke	1750	George Swaine
1402	William Shawe	1761	Robert Brydges
1403	William Aylward	1771	William Kymer
	Robert Catour	1794	Edward Foster
1427	Thomas Bronyng	1826	Aaron Foster
1444	Henry Martyn	1828	Charles James Cobley
1448	John Pedewel	1859	William Harkness
1467	Walter Osborn	1863	Richard Francis Follett
1484	John Wansforde	1895	John Alfred Dodd
1485	John Vele	1923	Herbert Cecil Sydenham
1520	Peter Carslegh	1930	Herbert Prior Boulton
1532	John Carselegh	1946	Walter Govett Tarr
1550	John Came	1960	William Lincoln Jones
1554	Robert Teynter	1971	Bernard Salmon
1556	John Bathon	1992	Ian Hubbard
1579	John Williams	1999	Michael Slade

* The 1650 Parliamentary Survey (S.R.O. DD/OB 33) lists
   Mr Lawrence Castle as the incumbent: a vicar not previously
   associated with Winscombe

BIBLIOGRAPHY

Alumni Oxoniensis, 1968   Alumni Oxoniensis Volume I, Kraus
Reprint Ltd, Nendeln, Liechtenstein, 474,

Alumni Cantabrigiensis, 1944   Alumni Cantabrigiensis Volume II,
Cambridge University Press, London, 79,

Alumni Cantabrigiensis, 1947   Alumni Cantabrigiensis Volume III,
Cambridge University Press, London, 245

Bettey, J H, 1979   Church and Community,
Moonraker Press, Bradford-on-Avon

Cal Pat Rolls, 1924   Calendar of Patent Rolls,
Edward VI, i, 1547-8, HMSO, London, 318-9

Cal Pat Rolls, 1925   Calendar of Patent Rolls,
Edward VI, iii, 1549-51, HMSO, London, 135

Cal Pat Rolls, 1926   Calendar of Patent Rolls,
Edward VI, iv, 1550-3, HMSO, London, 60

Clay, Mary Rotha, 1914   The Hermits and Anchorites of England,
Methuen, London, 246

Compton, Theodore, 1882   Winscombe Sketches,
William Poole, London, 45-47,

Compton, Theodore, 1892   A Mendip Valley,
Edward Stanford, London, 58-59

Crockfords Clerical Directory,   Crockfords Clerical Directory,
1874   Horace Cox, London, 302-3,

Crook, J Mordaunt, 1981   William Burges and the High Victorian Dream,
John Murray Ltd, London, 224,

Dale, W L, 1957   The Law of the Parish Church,
Butterworth & Co, London, 29

Dodd, R A, 1924   Some Winscombe Notes (unpublished)

Gilchrist, Roberta, 1995   Contemplation and Action, the Other
Monasticism, Leicester University Press

Green, Emanuel, 1888   Cardinal Pole's Pension Book 1553,
Somerset Record Society, Volume 2, 22

Green, Emanuel, 1888

Somerset Chantries, Surveys and Rentals, Somerset Record Society, Volume 2, 81-82, 263

HMC *Wells, 1907*

Calendar of the Manuscripts of the Dean and Chapter of Wells, Volume I, Ben Johnson & Co, York, 359, 361

HMC *Wells, 1914*

Calendar of the Manuscripts of the Dean and Chapter of Wells, Volume II, The Hereford Times Ltd, Hereford, 213

Hugo, Thomas, 1867

The Medieval Nunneries of the County of Somerset, J R Smith, London, 206

Jordan, Margaret, 1994

The Story of Compton Bishop and Cross, R A & M Jordan, Cross, 79

Knight, Francis A, 1915
(Reprinted 1971)

The Heart of Mendip, Chatford House Press Ltd, Bristol, 38, 44, 49, 51, 55

Liber Albus I and II

Liber Albus I and II, Wells Cathedral Library

Maxwell-Lyte, H C and
Dawes MCB, 1934

The Register of Thomas Bekynton, Bishop of Bath and Wells 1443-1465, Somerset Record Society Volume 49, 190

Paul, R W, 1882

Incised and Sepulchral Slabs of North-West Somerset, Provost & Co, London, 266

Scott-Holmes, Thomas, 1895

The Register of Ralph of Shrewsbury, Bishop of Bath and Wells 1329-1363, Somerset Record Society, Volume 9, 70

Shilton, Dorothy and
Holworthy, Richard, 1925

Medieval Wills from Wells, Somerset Record Society, Volume 40

Stewards Proposals Wells

Dean and Chapter of Wells Cathedral, Stewards Proposal Books, Volume 8, 68 (unpub)

Winscombe Vicarage, 1963

Particulars and Conditions of Sale of Winscombe Vicarage, W H Palmer and Sons

Woodforde, Christopher,
1946

Stained Glass in Somerset 1250-1830, Oxford University Press 149-154

Woodward, G H, 1982

Somerset Surveys and Rentals 1548-1603, Somerset Record Society, Volume 77, 1-2

SOMERSET RECORD OFFICE, TAUNTON
REFERENCES

DD/CC 10762	William White Map of Winscombe and Shipham, 1792
DD/CC 110733	Parliamentary Survey of the Manor of Winscombe, 1650
DD/CC 110735	Schedule for William White Map, Winscombe, 1792
DD/CC c/2208	Enclosure Award Map, Winscombe, 1799
DD/CTN 130, 131	Tithe Map and Award for Winscombe, 1840
DD/OB 33	Survey of the Parsonage or Rectory of Winscombe, 1650
DD/OB 39	Glebe Terrier of Winscombe, 1613
D/P/Winsc 9	Vestry Minute Books, Winscombe, 1741-1922
D/P/Winsc 13/2/1	Poor Rate Accounts, Winscombe, 1679-1714
D/P/Winsc 18/1/1	Charles Cobley Will, 1859

PUBLIC RECORD OFFICE, LONDON
REFERENCE

E 318	1823